Influence on the future Pedagogy, Psychology and Literature

By:

Umarqulova Diyora

Influence on the future : Pedagogy, Psychology and Literature
by: Umarqulova Diyora
Edition: August '2023
Publisher:
Taemeer Publications LLC (Michigan, USA / Hyderabad, India)

ISBN 978-93-5872-134-8
9 789358 721348

Book	:	***Influence on the future : Pedagogy, Psychology and Literature***
Author	:	Umarqulova Diyora
Publisher	:	Taemeer Publications
Year	:	'2023
Pages	:	96
Title Design	:	*Taemeer Web Design*

Table of Content

The impact of personality traits on the success of language learning

Abstract.:
Language learning is an interesting and important process that can open doors to new cultures and opportunities. However, success in language learning depends not only on teaching methods and materials, but also on the personal qualities of the student. In this article, we will look at the influence of personality traits such as extroversion, introversion, openness , closeness, self-esteem and inhibition on success in language learning.

Key words:
extroversion, introversion, language learning, openness, closeness, inhibition, self-esteem

Learning a language is a multifaceted process involving understanding grammar, vocabulary, pronunciation and the ability to communicate fluently in a new language. However, success in language acquisition does not depend only on educational materials and teaching methods. Personality traits play an important role in determining how effectively we can learn and master new languages.

Extroversion and success in language learning Extroversion is a personality trait characterized by sociality, activity and a tendency to communicate with other people. Research shows that extroverts are usually able to get inspired quickly and embark on new tasks, including language learning.

They can also easily communicate with native speakers, which can greatly improve their language skills. Extroverts usually easily make new acquaintances, feel comfortable in social situations and take the initiative in communication. These traits can have a positive impact on the language learning process. Extroverts, thanks to their sociability, often find language partners or groups to communicate, which helps them practice a new language and improve their skills. They can also easily participate in classroom discussions and communicate with teachers, which contributes to a deeper understanding of the language. They may also be bolder to make mistakes that don't greatly affect their self-esteem and mood. On the contrary, introverts are more reserved and may be afraid of communicating in an unfamiliar language.

Introversion and success in language learning

Introversion, unlike extroversion, is characterized by a preference for loneliness, internal orientation and caution in communication. Although introverts may find it harder to engage in social contacts, they have unique advantages when learning a language. Introverts often prefer deeper and more meaningful communication, which contributes to a more thorough study of grammar and language rules. Introverts, due to their propensity for self-reflection and internal processing of information, can be good observers and analysts of language. They often prefer a quieter learning environment where they can delve into learning materials without strong external distractions. Introverts usually listen more attentively and process information, which contributes to a deeper understanding of language and its subtleties.

Openness and success of language learning

Openness is another important personality trait that can affect the success of language learning. People with a high level of openness are usually more inclined to explore new ideas and concepts, which can be useful when learning a new language. They are often more resilient, and can spend more time learning and practicing, which can increase their level of language proficiency. Open personalities can also have advantages when learning a language. They tend to have new and diverse experiences and are more inclined to try new things, which may include learning a new language. They are often interested in other cultures and may be more motivated to learn a language in order to better understand other cultures.

Closeness and success of language learning Closeness is a personality trait characterized by a tendency to conservative views and a reduced openness to new experiences. In the context of language learning, closeness can be an obstacle. However, it is worth noting that each individual is unique, and some closed people may show high motivation and perseverance when learning a language. Closed personalities may experience great caution and preference for familiar situations and communication with loved ones. This can make it difficult for them to learn a new language, especially in the context of communication and practice. However, thanks to a systematic and methodical approach, closed personalities can have advantages when learning a language, such as deeper immersion in the topic being studied and systematic assimilation of language rules.

Self-esteem and success of language learning

How someone sees and values themselves as an individual can be used to describe self-esteem. This has a lot to do with the concept of self-concept, which is how someone perceives themselves in terms of their emotional, physical, spiritual, and social selves, as well as a variety of other aspects. A language learner's sense of self-worth is crucial. It concerns how a language student sees himself or herself, whether that person sees themselves as a successful or unsuccessful language learner.

The primary authors who have contributed to the development of the theoretical idea of self-esteem include James (1890), White (1959), Coopersmith (1959 and 1967), Rosenberg (1965 and 1979), Branden (1969 and 1994), and Mruk (1999 and 2006). Their descriptions essentially highlight six key elements or dimensions of self-esteem:

- Competence and worthiness
- Cognition and affect
- Consistency and openness

Listyani (2004) conducted a research in an English Education Study Program of a private university in Central Java, Indonesia. She discovered that self- esteem has a positive and significant effect on the students' English proficiency with a score of 88.36%.

Self-esteem can have a significant impact on success in learning a language. Here are some examples:

- High self-esteem can help a student feel more confident and become more motivated. He will speak the language more often, it is easier to endure failures, setting higher goals for himself and striving for a better result.

- Low self-esteem, on the contrary, can cause a student to fear and fear of mistakes, avoiding participation in conversations and lessons, which will accordingly affect his success in learning the language.

- Self-esteem can also affect how well a student performs exercises and assignments in grammar, reading, writing and speech comprehension.

- In some cases, high self-esteem can lead to a reassessment of their knowledge and skills in the language, which can lead to seeming perfection, which can harm their development and language learning.

Therefore, although high self-esteem can be useful for success, it should not lead to underestimation and substitution of views of experienced teachers and classmates. In addition, knowing how to properly evaluate your own efforts and how to make mistakes will help you learn the language successfully, without compromising self-esteem.

Inhibition and success of language learning

Inhibition is a state in which a person or group of students fear making a fool of themselves, worry about making mistakes, and avoid eye contact when speaking (Ur, 1996, p. 121). Others have noted that inhibition relates to a temperamental predisposition to show wariness, fearfulness, or restraint in response to strange people, objects, and situations (Kagan et al., 1988). These explain how inhibition has an impact on pupils' language learning, particularly when it comes to language understanding.

Inhibition or a general lack of self-confidence and one's abilities can negatively affect language learning. Here are a few reasons why this might happen:

- Lack of confidence can cause stress and anxiety in the student, which can lead to the fact that he will not speak the language as often as he should. This in turn may make it difficult for him to improve his language skills.

- If a student feels inhibited due to his uncertainty, he may find it difficult to understand the teacher or other students who speak the language. This can greatly slow down the learning process for him.

- Lack of confidence can lead to the fact that the student will begin to avoid difficult, but important exercises for him. For example, he may avoid learning complex grammatical constructions or learning new words because he is afraid of mistakes or failure.

- Lack of confidence can also prevent a student from integrating into the classroom and communicating with other students, which can make it difficult to practice speaking the language and getting feedback.

It is important to understand that these personality traits represent only one aspect of the impact on success in language learning. Other factors such as motivation, teaching methods and the learning environment also play an important role. Each personality is unique, and different approaches and strategies can be effective for different types of personalities. Therefore, it is important to create a supportive and inclusive educational environment that takes into account the diversity of personality traits and provides students with opportunities for successful language learning.

References:

- James, W. 1983. (Ed. 1890). The principles of psychology, Cambridge: Harvard University Press.
- Kagan, et all. (1988). Childhood derivatives in inhibition and lack of inhibition to the unfamiliar. Child Development, 59, 1580-1589.
- Listyani. (2022). The importance of self-esteem in the language learning journey: Procedural writing students' stories in Indonesia. European Journal of English Language Studies, 2(2), 47-59. https://doi.org/10.12973/ejels.2.2.47
- Mruk, C. 1999 (2 ed.). Self-esteem: Research, theory and practice, New York: Single Publishing Company. 2006 (3 ed.). Self-esteem Research, theory and practice. New York: Single Publishing Company.
- Ur, P. (1996). A course in Language teaching: Practice and theory. UK: Cambridge University Press.
- https://blog.thelinguist.com/introverts-vs-extroverts/

Meaningful organization of youth leisure and popularization of sports

Abstract:
Youth is the main engine of social progress and development. Young people have inexhaustible energy, ambition and the potential to achieve great results. In this article we will discuss the role of sport in the lives of young people and why it plays a key role in their physical, psychological and social development. In addition, it is considered how much our state pays attention to the leisure of young people and their interest in sports.

Key words:
sport, youth, health, development, sport clubs

Youth sports offer various chances for a physically active lifestyle, which is crucial for healthy and optimal development throughout childhood and early adulthood. Increasing children's wellbeing at this period can also benefit your community's future because youngsters who take part in these activities are better adjusted as adults with a wealth of life experience and learning under their belts.

Physical health and well-being: Participation in sports contributes to maintaining a healthy lifestyle among young people. Regular physical training helps strengthen the immune system, increase endurance and strength, as well as improve coordination and flexibility. This helps prevent a number of diseases associated with lack of movement, such as obesity, cardiovascular diseases and diabetes. Sport also helps to relieve stress and improve mood, which is important for the overall physical and emotional well-being of young people.

Developing skills and character:

Participation in sports events develops skills that are an integral part of a successful life. Young people learn to work in a team, set and achieve goals, overcome difficulties and develop leadership skills. They will learn about the importance of discipline, patience and perseverance in achieving success. These skills are transferred from sports to other areas of life, including education, career and personal relationships.

Social integration and value formation:

Sport is an excellent means of social integration of young people. It unites people of different ages, nationalities and social groups around a common goal. Sports teams and clubs become a place where young people find support, friendship and mutual understanding. They also learn the values of fair play, impartiality and respect for rivals. By doing sports, young people learn to work in a team, make decisions and resolve conflicts, which contributes to their social adaptation and the development of communication skills. Sport also provides young people with the opportunity to get to know different cultures and traditions. International competitions and sports exchanges allow young people to meet with representatives of other countries, exchange experiences and learn about the differences and similarities between cultures. This contributes to their tolerance, openness and global thinking.

Turning a hobby into a professional career:

For some young people, sport becomes a professional vocation. Participation in sports teams and the training program open doors for them to sports universities and professional leagues. This allows young people to develop their potential, achieve high results and do what they love at a professional level.

Sport in Uzbekistan

In Uzbekistan, every opportunity is provided for both boys and girls to grow up in harmony and to acquire a high-quality education.Large-scale reforms are being implemented in this area, and novel advancements are being put into practice.President Shavkat Mirziyoyev learned about projects in the areas of youth, sports, healthcare, and the electric power business on January 30 in 2022 as a result.

Large-scale efforts have been made recently to reinforce the state youth policy's legal basis. Projects and initiatives are being carried out to educate people with a sound worldview and independent thought. The study of and dissemination to the populace of the rich spiritual heritage of great thinkers, as well as the preservation of national traditions and values, are given special consideration. On January 19, 2022, the President issued the Decree titled "On measures to radically improve the system of working with youth in mahallas." The document was adopted in an effort to further boost the effectiveness of spiritual, educational, and educational work in educational institutions as well as to introduce new mechanisms for managing work with youth, develop a vertical system of work with boys and girls, and solve their problems directly on the ground. On January 25, 2022, the Law "On Amendments to Some Legislative Acts of the Republic of Uzbekistan in Connection with the Improvement of the System of Work with Youth" was adopted. As a result, the Agency for Youth Affairs is now a part of the state bodies that report violations of minors' rights, freedoms, and legitimate interests to the appropriate authorities as well as identify minors and families who are in need of social assistance.

It is necessary to take a number of measures to popularize sports among young people. Some of them are listed below:

1. Creation of free sports clubs for young people in schools, universities, parks and other public places. This will help make sports accessible and attractive to everyone.

2. Organization of sports events and competitions that can attract the attention of young people. It can be either a large-scale event, or a small tournament or match.

3. Advertising campaigns promoting a healthy lifestyle and regular physical activity. Such campaigns can be carried out both on television and radio, as well as on social networks and other online services.

4. Cooperation with influential personalities to attract interest in sports. These can be both professional athletes and celebrities who are actively involved in sports.

5. Creation of programs to support and encourage young people involved in sports. These can be scholarships, prizes and other types of encouragement for achievements in sports.

6. The inclusion of sports activities and exercises in school curricula, so that children from an early age begin to be interested in sports and know about its importance for health.

7. Creation of special applications and services that will help young people choose a sport suitable for them and engage in it regularly.

Sport plays an integral role in the lives of young people, giving them the opportunity to develop physically, emotionally and socially. This contributes to the maintenance of health, character development and the formation of values. In addition, sports can become the basis for a further professional career. Therefore, it is important to encourage and support young people in their sports efforts, creating conditions for their participation in various sports events and training programs. Sport gives young people the opportunity to realize their potential and become active and successful participants in society. I think that the state should pay attention to the development of sports youth, as sports always helps to prevent a number of diseases. Our state supports young athletes, and not only them, but also musicians, artists, everyone who is engaged in art, who spends their time with meaning.

References:

1. https://nationalacademyofathletics.com/engaging-in-sports-has-many-benefits-for-young-people/
2. https://yuz.uz/ru/news/vozmojnosti-dlya-samorealizatsii

Mastering Time Management: Strategies for Students Balancing Work and Studies

Abstract:

The article discusses the problems associated with time management in the life of students. Time management is the formation of students basic knowledge of theoretical foundations and practical skills in the field of time management as an intangible resource, which are the basis for organizing effective activities both at the personal and corporate level.

Key words:

setting goals, time management, career development, self-discovery

Introduction

Every individual on earth has the same amount of time - 60 seconds in a minute; 60 minutes in an hour; 1,440 minutes in a day; and 525,600 minutes in a year. While a vast majority of people confesses faltering to come to grips with it, extremely few can claim to have made the most of it. How is it that they have got it all done? It's because they have managed a way to figure out how to manage their time effectively1.

Time management is the act or process of exercising conscious control over the time spent on specific activities in order to specifically increase efficiency and productivity. Time management can help you develop a range of skills, tools, and

---

1 Dr Sharma S. Mantha. Handbook on Time Management Skills.

techniques to help you complete specific tasks, projects, and goals. This set includes a wide range of activities, namely: planning, allocation, goal setting, delegation, time analysis, monitoring, organizing, listing and prioritization2.

Literature review

Student time is continuously a time of tests on life, all sorts of trial and blunder, and self-discovery. Some individuals give themselves totally to their studies. Someone is attempting to combine it with work. Time administration tips for students will assist you to organize your time accurately in arrange to oversee to manage with both the educational modules and the work assignment, and still have time to relax. Often we listen “oh, in case there were more hours within the day” or “I would have 25 hours a day, I would have done everything”. And individuals who achieve much more within the same 24 hours are admired. It is the capacity to oversee your time and undertakings that is mindful for the individual efficiency of each person. Young people in their life are guided by the proverb «Take everything from life! ». Today there are numerous openings for the realization of their thoughts and desires. It remains as it were to get it how to combine work and consider, so that there's still an opportunity without regret to spend the arranged excursion in a curiously way.

Many students who have arranged career development begin working during their studies. And usually a shrewd choice to pickup proficient involvement indeed sometime recently getting to be a specialist. Such specialists have continuously been and will be in incredible demand.

---

2 https://ru.wikipedia.org/wiki/Управление_временем

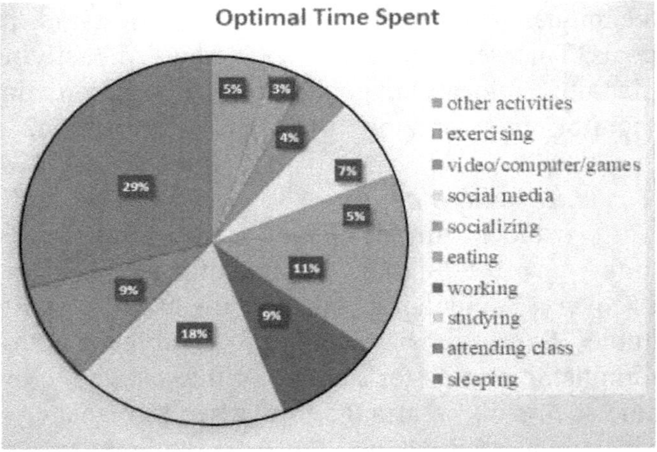

Рисунок 1. Optimal Time Spent for Students

Form of think about and work: discover a fruitful duet.

The easiest way to combine work and think about is in the event that you're an understudy of correspondence, evening or separate learning. For full-time understudies, this assignment gets to be a few times more difficult. It is exceptionally great in case they were able to concur on such a person plan for going to classes, and the instructor went forward. In most cases, the issue of combination requires other solutions. If you discover your dependable company, get counsel and clarifications from it on the work performed, take an interest in composing them, at that point you'll be able adapt with the preparing program without debt.

Find your work option.

The moment arrangement to the effective organization of working time can be the choice of a reasonable choice for work whereas studying.

Work with adaptable hours or shift. This organize permits, after analyzing the course plan, to select a helpful work schedule.

Work within the evenings. So, you'll be able go to classes amid the day, and within the evening, by understanding with the employer, do work. True, the educational programs can also influence the evening hours, so you would like to choose which ones you'll skip and which ones you ought to not.

Internships. They permit not only to win cash (frequently not paid), but around the work of diverse masters, to get it whether the chosen forte suits you. It is additionally an opportunity to display yourself to a potential employer. This could be a great alternative to

urge important viable encounter without ruining relations with the instructing staff. Since numerous colleges, like companies, organize internships for understudies themselves.

Time administration standards: basic rules

for troublesome tasks We see that there are ways to keep considers going and offer

assistance discover an understanding between instruction and work. However, this is often not precisely what we are interested in. The primary thing is to memorize how to combine them so merely can do everything else. And here you would like information and strict execution of the fundamental standards of time administration for understudies.

The rule of advance. Try to carefully arrange the most occasions of the following month. Separate working and end of the week days, check critical occasions, due dates for completing work on the curriculum. Schedule the up and coming week essentially hourly, showing the term of occasions and free time.

The rule of recording events. All arranging must be set on a few mediums, and not kept within the head. Such a carrier can be a week after week diary, note pad, arranging, versatile application on the phone or an extraordinary program on the computer. The data will be presented outwardly and it'll be simpler to analyze it, make changes and not miss anything.

The rule of parallelism. It is necessary to memorize when performing activities that don't require concentration and action from you, to do something else. For illustration, on the way to work or school, you'll be able grant addresses, do homework, learn outside dialects, and so on. It is imperative to be able to require advantage of such a circumstance and the comes about will not be long in coming.

The main assistant in the organization of the student's educational activities can be time management (TM) - a separate direction of management aimed specifically at solving the problems of time organization. Time management of a university student is a systematic, consistent and purposeful use of a set of mastered techniques for organizing personal and educational activities in everyday practice in order to increase the effectiveness of self-organization. This technology forms a value attitude to time, the phenomenon of self-organization, the learning process. For effective time management, there are many methods and principles of time management, using which you can learn how to effectively manage time. Time management includes a wide range of activities, including:

- setting goals;
- time planning and allocation;
- making lists;
- prioritization;
- time cost analysis, etc.

The absence of at least minimal planning and organization in life leads to an inefficient expenditure of energy, money and time by a person, and the output turns out that the day passes in a rush, and nothing is really done, stress and fatigue arise, dissatisfaction with oneself grows. The task of time management is to save a person from inefficient waste of an invaluable resource – time. Think about what you do, who you communicate with, what you spend precious minutes on. You can't learn manage time and at the same time do not value your own and other people's time.

Without a plan, reaching your goals tends to be a hit-or-miss proposition, and time is easily wasted. Without a plan, you may find yourself reacting to the demands of others rather than focusing on your own goals. Without a plan, you will miss the benefits that come from using effective planning skills. Before considering the benefits of effective planning, perform the self-audit on the next page, and identify your strengths and areas for improvement with regard to planning.

Objective setting is incomprehensible without planning. To accomplish assignments, an individual must arrange certain actions. The result will be fruitful as it were with a clear step-by-step execution of them. At the introductory organize, arranging will not be able to require into consideration all the subtleties, hence, it is conditional3.

Five minutes' rest in studying process. The optimal mode is 5 minutes of rest every hour. Maybe 10 minutes in an hour and a half. Duration from an hour to an hour and a half is the most

---

3 Умаркулова, Д.С. Целеполагание / Д.С. Умаркулова. — Текст: электронный // NovaInfo, 2022. — № 131. — URL: https://novainfo.ru/article/19073 (дата обращения: 09.04.2022).

comfortable interval for a person for continuous work. Remember school and university: a lesson is 45 minutes, a "pair" is an hour and a half. No matter how busy the working day is, highlight these 5 minutes. Invest time in five minutes of rest, work without them is extremely inefficient.4

The key time management points:

- ✓ Recognize your responsibilities and be proactive at work instead of being reactive.
- ✓ Always have a clear goal in mind: "Don't work hard to get up the ladder and at the top discover that it's leaning against the wrong wall."
- ✓ Prioritize your tasks: Focus on the important tasks which can be scheduled and planned in advance, not on the urgent, unexpected ones. Do the first things first.
- ✓ Nurture your relationships with a "win-win" approach to tense situations.
- ✓ Be a good listener and focus on understanding before being understood. Use empathetic listening to genuinely understand the person you are talking to5.

Time is an irreplaceable and non-renewable resource. It is your most valuable asset. It cannot be accumulated and its losses cannot be restored. Everything you do takes time. The better you use it, the more you will achieve and the greater the dividends will be6.

---

4 Gleb Arkhangelsky. Time-Drive. How to Have Time to Live and to Work, 2005.

5 Stephen R. Covey. The 7 Habits of Highly Effective People: Powerful Lessons in Personal Change,1989.

6 Brian Tracy. Time Management: The Brian Tracy Success Library, 2006.

Conclusion

Remember that you can lose time, but you can invest wisely. Investing time in time management is not a cost, but an investment. Successful people differ in that they allocate enough time to invest in your future.

References:

- Brian Tracy. Time Management: The Brian Tracy Success Library, 2006.
- Dr Sharma S. Mantha. Handbook on Time Management Skills.

- Gleb Arkhangelsky. Time-Drive. How to Have Time to Live and to Work, 2005.
- https://ru.wikipedia.org/wiki/Управление_временем
- Stephen R. Covey. The 7 Habits of Highly Effective People: Powerful Lessons in Personal Change,1989.

- Умаркулова, Д.С. Целеполагание / Д.С. Умаркулова. — Текст: электронный // NovaInfo, 2022. — № 131. — URL: https://novainfo.ru/article/19073 (дата обращения: 09.04.2022).

JACK LONDON IN SEARCH OF THE IDEAL : THE CULT NOVEL "MARTIN EDEN"

Annotation:

The article is devoted to the work of Jack London "Martin Eden". It is established that the tragic discrepancy between reality and the romantic idealization of ideas and personalities becomes the key source of the plot conflict, which leads the protagonist to subsequent disappointment in ideals and loss of life orientations. The main cause of the hero's tragedy is spiritual loneliness, the reckoning that overtakes the one who dares to rise too high, to think too boldly. The article contains such components as a summary, subject matter and description of the main characters of the novel.

Key words:

Jack London, main character, literature, novel, subject matter, philosophy

Introduction

Jack London lived a truly superhuman life. For 16 years of his literary activity, he wrote 50 books, countless articles, traveled all over America with lectures on socialism as a perfect form of world order, did not refuse a single person who asked him for help ... With all the passion of his nature, he tried to materialize three his great illusions: marriage "on a reasonable basis" with healthy offspring, socialism and the theory of the superman. "Reasonable marriage" took revenge on him by alienating his daughters; socialism - by setting fire to his "House of the Wolf", and he parted with the third illusion himself. Jack London was a man of arbitrary decisions - a materialist. When life began to leave the body and he no longer felt like a superman, he killed his spirit.

Literature review

Brief summary. Cheerful young sailor Martin Eden by chance meets the wealthy Morse family. And discovers the world of culture, beauty, books. In love with Ruth Morse, he writes poetry and prose, dreams of becoming a famous writer. He believes in his talent. Hard work earns a living, reads, writes. But everyone advises him to find a normal job. In the end, even Ruth breaks off her engagement to him. And the poet's best friend takes his own life. He, disappointed, suddenly finds glory. Money and honor surround the young writer. And Ruth is ready to become his wife. But in his soul something died. Life is no longer happy. And Martin Eden commits suicide at the moment when the ship carries him to the beautiful islands. He jumps into the water and drowns7.

Time of creation of the work, main problem, theme and idea. Jack London's famous novel Martin Eden was first published in 1908-1909 in Pacific Mansley. In 1909, the novel was published as a separate book. This work, which tells about the intellectual development of Martin Eden, a talented individualist, turned out to be largely autobiographical. The

---

7 Valery Viktorovich Andreev. Analysis of the work of Jack London "Martin Eden" // Educational portal "Reference book". — Date of last update of the article: 04/17/2022. — URLhttps://spravochnick.ru/literatura/literatura_ssha/analiz_proizvedeniya_dzheka_londona_martin_iden/ (date of access: 07.12.2022).

action of the work begins in two directions, interconnected: the protagonist's love for Ruth and his struggle for a place in society, the struggle for society to finally recognize Martin's writing talent. Jack London in his novel raises the following topics:

1. Love Theme ;
2. Society Theme ;
3. The theme of education ;
4. Aspiration Theme ;
5. Humanity Theme ;
6. The theme of self-improvement.

The theme of love is one of the main themes of the work. It is this theme that is fundamental in London's novel. "Martin Eden" is a work of a romantic nature, and therefore the essence of the relationship between the characters is either love or hate. And it happens that a person himself cannot fully understand what kind of feeling attracts him to another person - this is evidenced by the position of Ruth. Society is presented to the reader as the absolute opposite of the protagonist of the novel, and this especially clearly reflects his inner world, his essence. Ruth, the heroine of London's work, is the personification of the bourgeois class. And Martin Eden is a bright representative of the working class, but he was able to set himself a goal and strive for it, regardless of what level of the social hierarchy he is at. At the time of the creation of the novel, it was believed that if a person belongs to the bourgeois class, then he is smart, educated and well-read, and this is a distinctive feature of people of this class. However, Jack London in his novel shows that his hero, being lower in terms of wealth, turned out to be much smarter than the representatives of the bourgeois class. If for them knowledge was a matter of course, then Eden strives for it himself8.

Another theme touched upon in the novel "Martin Eden" is the theme of aspiration. The protagonist of the novel can be called one of the most purposeful heroes of the work. first of all, striving is overcoming oneself, and this is clearly seen in the example of Martin Eden. In the novel, on the opposition of the protagonist with society, the writer shows another theme - the theme of humanity. Martin always tries to help his sister, friends and loved ones. He even helped a complete stranger, and he, for fun, invited him to visit him so that his relatives would look at a person from a lower society. Jack London in the novel raises such problems as unrequited love, the problem of the empty upper class of society, the problem of access to education for representatives of the working class, the problem of a person's lack of striving for the best, for achieving success. The author also raises the problem of the fact that not every person is ready to help another, which is relevant at all times.

Genre, plot, composition of the novel, its artistic features. "Martin Eden"

refers to the genre of the novel. A pronounced autobiographical element lends credibility to the novel. In the work, the echoes of the life story of the protagonist of the work with the biography of the author himself are obvious. The story takes place in Auckland in the early 20th century. The protagonist of the novel, Martin Eden, is a simple working guy,

8 https://litra.bobrodobro.ru/1759

a native of the lower classes, a sailor, who accidentally met a girl from a wealthy family, Ruth Morse. The guy fell in love with her at first sight, and wanting to become worthy of the girl, he actively takes up self-improvement. Ruth sees in Martin a "savage" and takes patronage over his undertakings. Martin is determined to become a writer, he is sure that he can write much better than the authors of works published in literary magazines. Martin works on his pronunciation and language, reads a lot, begins to write poetry and prose. Over time, he becomes an experienced writer, but the years go by, and success never comes. Ruth realizes that she has fallen in love with Martin, but her parents do not approve of their daughter's choice, but still decide not to openly interfere with their engagement. They try in every possible way to present Eden as unworthy in the eyes of Ruth, they invite accomplished young people to the house.

Eden's book, which one publisher dared to publish, caused a sensation. The longawaited success comes to Martin, but it does not bring him satisfaction. Martin is constantly invited to banquets, dinners, filled with offers and letters. Ruth herself comes to Martin, now no longer a poor hard worker, but a fashionable and wealthy writer, and offers her hand and heart. However, Martin realizes that his feelings have faded and refuses her. The hero suddenly realizes that he does not need this fame, he does not need big money. He decides to buy a small island in the Pacific Ocean and hide there from the hustle and bustle. The composition of Jack London's novel is distinguished by simplicity and harmony. The center of the composition is the image of the protagonist, not a single event in the novel can do without his participation. The core of the plot is the evolution of the personality of the heroartist, his driving force. And the centripetal construction of the composition provides an opportunity to achieve maximum concentration of attention on the inner world of the hero and on the work that is constantly going on in his soul.

Characteristics of the main characters. Jack London, working on the novel Martin Eden, included a whole list of heroes to reveal the problems of the work. Here we meet Ruth Morse, whom Martin fell in love with. However, the heroine herself could not reciprocate him. For her, Martin is just a hobby. Maybe for this reason she did not believe that Martin Eden would become a worthy writer. I would like to highlight among the characters of the novel Lizzie Connolly, who loved the main character very much, and was with him from the same class. Moreover, Lizzie loved him as a person, and not his fame or money. The only pity is that due to mental illness, Martin does not stay with Lizzie. The novel also features such characters as Professor Caldwell, who had an invaluable influence on the main character and became the first intellectual on the path of Martin. Here are Russ Brissenden - a friend of the hero, his sisters with their husbands, and Maria Silva, from whom Martin rented an apartment. However, among all the characters, it is Martin Eden who remains the main character. We will talk about him and his image. The main character of the novel is Martin Eden - a representative of the working class, a sailor. He is bold, full of energy and strength, open to new knowledge, self-confident and purposeful. Martin is hardy, able to sleep several hours a day, devoting the rest of the time to work. He always keeps his word, strives to help those in need. Feel free to express your opinion. Martin can stand up for himself and for his loved ones. Love for Ruth changed a lot in him, thanks to this feeling he began to change both externally and internally. Many of the positive features of the former Martin remained with him, but refinement of manners, accuracy, rejection of bad habits were added to them, speech became more literate and refined. But there is also a downside to Martin's character. He is an individualist, puts personal interests above the public. Ruth Morse is the beloved of the protagonist, Bachelor of Arts. However, at its core, the girl is an ordinary bourgeois, unable to accept life. She is an imaginary representative of the reflective intelligentsia. But Ruth is not a negative character - she has a lot of sincere, kind, bright. She helps Martin, sincerely feels sorry for Lizzy. The image of the heroine is ambiguous, since her environment is largely to blame.

Main character. Martin Eden is the protagonist of the novel. He is a twentyyear-old uneducated young man. He is poor, uncouth, but he has a strong will and habit of work. Martin lost his parents early, so he had to earn a living by the hard work of a sailor. Martin rents a cramped room in his sister's house, but this miserable closet can barely fit a bed, washbasin and one chair. The hero's relationship with his son-in-law does not add up, who reproaches him for drunkenness and dependency. The turning point in Martin's life is visiting family Mr Morse.

A noble bourgeois invites the young man to dinner in gratitude for the service rendered: Martin stood up for the honor of his son. Having been in an intelligent house, where he was first called “Mister”, having met his love there - “a pale airy creature”, Martin lights up with the desire to overcome the barrier between himself and “people of high culture”. London's novel is full of contrasts. It sharply contrasts each other with the world of battlers, morses and higginbothams (the world of

American philistinism, from large prosperous businessmen to miserable townsfolk who dream of being like them) and the world of working people, represented primarily by Martin Eden, his friends, Lizzy Connolly, participants in crowd scenes. At the will of the author, the reader finds himself either in Morse's salon, or in the laundry room where the main character works, in his cramped closet, where, choking on the smoke of a kerosene stove, he writes his first poems and stories, reads book after book, mastering the treasures of world culture, and also intoxicating ideas from the books of trendy decadent authors. Martin begins to get acquainted with the philosophy of Spencer and Nietzsche after the beloved of the young writer Ruth sharply criticizes his work. Reading Spencer's writings, Martin discovers that "once he knew nothing ... that he only skimmed the surface of things without any attempt to establish a connection between them." A radical restructuring of the hero's worldview takes place, he acquires the ability to abstract, move away from reality, and leaves his former existence. Martin becomes a famous and highly paid writer9.

But he doesn't feel happy. In the world of Morses and Battlers, feelings turn out to be false (Ruth is only passionate about Martin, their relationship is just a game for her). Martin is experiencing a break with the former environment - the environment of working people capable of sincere feelings (Lizzy Connolly's love for Martin) of Martin is tragic. In this hero, the features of a new person are noticeable, who is replacing people whose souls have been crippled by the world of possessive relationships. The talent of the young writer contains a new perception of the world. Martin was born and

---

9 https://lit.ukrtvory.ru/tragediya-martina-idena-po-romanu-dzh-londona

raised by the working people, carries his morality, his understanding of reality.

Martin has an amazing sense of purpose and faith in his own strength - he goes to the goal alone, hearing only reproaches, not finding any approval, even the bride does not believe in him. However, he achieves recognition, he proves that he is capable of the impossible. But this strong man has no support left, and he seems to be collapsing under his own weight. Disappointed and in the fashionable philosophical trends at that time, never having been religious, Martin Eden has absolutely nowhere to look for support, renewal10.

At the same time, the author himself, having gone through a difficult school of working life, is far from sugary admiration for people from the people who pave the way to art. And this goal can be achieved only with great demands on oneself, at the cost of hard work, opening access to knowledge that others - like young Morses - got easily, as they received them in privileged schools. However, it is hard for Martin to be in the world from which he has achieved recognition, he has nothing to breathe surrounded by philistines and businessmen, he is not attracted by comfort and convenience, in addition, he has lost both his friend and his lover. Martin dooms himself to voluntary death. He makes the last orders: he ensures a comfortable existence for the sisters, and he also does not forget to thank Maria, the landlady of the apartment he rents,

---

10 Осьмухина Ольга Юрьевна, Танасейчук Андрей Борисович Трагедия художника в романе Дж. Лондона "Мартин Иден" // Филологические науки. Вопросы теории и практики. 2018. №11-2 (89). URL: https://cyberleninka.ru/article/n/tragediya-hudozhnika-v-romane-dzh-londona-martin-iden (дата обращения: 18.02.2023).

for her kind, cordial attitude. Martin merges with the ocean - a powerful natural element that symbolizes the environment from which he came out, where the roots lie that nourished his skill.

Conclusion

Plunging into philosophy during self-education, Martin was just afraid that the form would prevail over the idea, over the content, over the very essence. Both hearts in love were held hostage by formalities and restrictions, despite all the romance and sincerity. From the point of view of love relationships, the result, of course, is sad, but if we rely on creativity and the highest aspirations in life, we understand that sometimes even a small powerful push in the form of the most sincere and mutual feelings, even a small spark can ignite the all-consuming flame of self-development, spiritual and physical self-improvement.

References:

- ✓ Valery Viktorovich Andreev. Analysis of the work of Jack London "Martin Eden" // Educational portal "Reference book". — Date of last update of the article: 04/17/2022. — URLhttps://spravochnick.ru/literatura/literatura_ssha/analiz_proizvedeniya_dzheka_londona_martin_iden/ (date of access: 07.12.2022).
- ✓ https://artifex.ru/
- ✓ https://lit.ukrtvory.ru/tragediya-martina-idena-po-romanu-dzh-londona
- ✓ https://litra.bobrodobro.ru/1759

✓ Осьмухина Ольга Юрьевна, Танасейчук Андрей Борисович Трагедия художника в романе Дж. Лондона "Мартин Иден" // Филологические науки. Вопросы теории и практики. 2018. №11-2 (89). URL: https://cyberleninka.ru/article/n/tragediya-hudozhnika-v-romane-dzh-londona-martin-iden (дата обращения: 18.02.2023).

The role of intrinsic motivation in second language acquisition among adult learners

Abstract:

This article discusses definitions such as "motivation" and "intrinsic motivation" and their role in learning a foreign language by adult learners. As well as four stages of language learning by adult learners.

Key words:

motivation, intrinsic motivation, adult learner, motive

The formation of motivation among students is one of the central and fundamental problems of modern society, as well as the problem of both domestic and foreign psychology. Its significance is connected with the analysis of the sources of human activity, the motivating forces of his activity, behavior.

For many years, the question of motivation has been the subject of research by teachers and scientists.

The term "motivation" in modern psychology can mean at least two mental phenomena: 1) a set of motives that cause and determine the activity, behavior of an individual; 2) the process of formation, the formation of motives that supports the activity of behavior, human activity at a certain level.

According to R.S. Nemov, motivation can be defined as "a set of psychological reasons that explain human behavior, its origin, orientation and activity."

Motivation is an internal psychological characteristic of a person, which finds expression in external manifestations, in a person's attitude to the world around him, various types of activities. Motivation appears when a person needs certain information or skills, which can only be obtained by changing the existing knowledge system.

As for intrinsic motivation, this is a psychological state of a person. It does not depend on material benefits, and is aimed at the self-development of the employee and the realization of his potential.

An example of intrinsic motivation is : participation in corporate events, because to take a lot of new and useful things for yourself.

The main task of motivation for learning is the organization of such educational events that maximize the inner potential of the personality of students. And here an important role is played by the choice of forms of organization of educational activities. The teacher needs to create a situation in which all students feel their involvement and respond from the teacher himself. Educational tasks should be formed directly based on the interests and requests of students, and the result should meet their needs, be meaningful, then students themselves will take the initiative, will strive to find an answer to a question or a solution to a problem. According to research, the main motives for learning a foreign language are the opportunity to communicate with native speakers, read foreign literature and get a position in an international company abroad. However, many students note a decrease in motivation after two or three months of study. Such a phenomenon, as experts in the field of methodology explain, may be due to the monotony of tasks, the overload of students with information or the inability of the teacher to properly organize the educational process. The main type of internal motivation is communicative motivation. Naturally, most foreign language learners want to communicate with native speakers, would like to work in a foreign corporation and directly use a new language in professional practice. Despite this trend, it is this type of motivation that we retain to the least extent. In the atmosphere of the native language, the mastery of a foreign language is presented as an artificial means of communication, and as a result, the situations used in teaching are artificial. Regardless of how the teacher tries to create a natural situation for communication, language remains an artificial component of this situation. This means that you need to use your imagination and play form more often. As part of university studies, a role-playing or business game is conducted. Games turn even a monotonous topic into a lively, interesting activity.

Adults have an intrinsic motivation to study, most often it is aimed at achieving social and professional goals. And unlike a child, an adult has a rich life experience and an idea of how to do the right thing and how not to. This can both help and hinder learning.

Connie Malamed, a distance education specialist, talks about the characteristics of an adult student:

1. Autonomy. Adult students prefer to independently control the learning process. They like to make choices while studying. Even adults who initially experience

anxiety during independent work will learn to enjoy it — with sufficient support from the curator.

2. Experience and knowledge. The peculiarity of an adult student is that he already has some knowledge, as well as a unique experience. All this is brought into the learning process and affects it.
3. Focus on the results. Adults, unlike children, more often understand the specific goals of their education. They know why they need new skills and what benefits they will get from knowledge.
4. The presence of responsibilities. Adult students, in addition to studying, have many household responsibilities — family, work and social. It is not always easy to allocate time for training in the daily routine.
5. The need for community. Many of those who study independently prefer to do it in the company. You can discuss study issues with like-minded people, including the difficulties of self-motivation.

According to the Kolb model, the adult education program should consist of four stages:

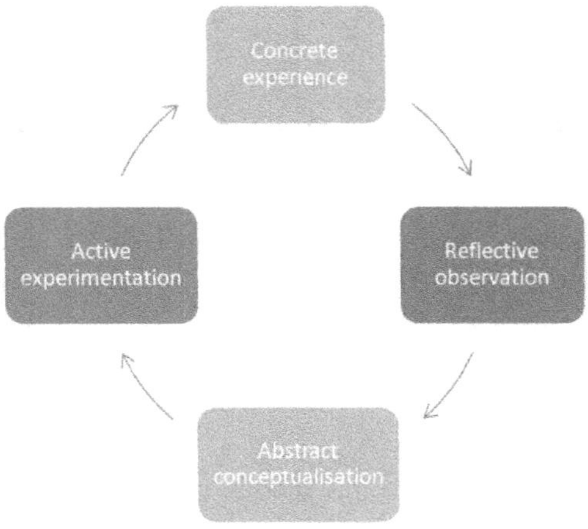

Training can begin at any stage. For example, some people start this process with theory or reflection. According to this principle, there are 4 types of people. Activists begin by gaining experience through trial and error, thinkers — first think and then act, theorists — by studying theoretical data, and pragmatists — by applying new knowledge in practice. There may be participants in the study group who prefer different styles, so the training program should include tasks that are attractive to everyone.

In conclusion, the motivation of adult students to learn a foreign language is the most important methodological problem that requires attention from the teacher. Only the joint efforts of each of the links of this complex multi-level system can give positive results. Organizational and methodological conditions of motivation are based on the life experience of students, the priority of independent work, individualization of learning, its activity nature, etc. Thus, the teacher must do everything possible to ensure that motivation develops and does not fade throughout the entire course of foreign language teaching. Of course, this is quite a difficult task, because for this the teacher needs to know the preferences, tastes and interests of his students, to know which side to approach and how to "warm up" motivation. In such cases, the teacher can be helped by increasing motivation to learn a foreign language.

References:

- ✓ Dzilikhova L.F., Andieva S.E. THE SIGNIFICANCE OF MOTIVATION IN LEARNING FOREIGN LANGUAGES // Modern science-intensive technologies. - 2016. - No. 1. - P. 97-101; URL:https://top-technologies.ru/ru/article/view?id=35500 (date of access: 05/20/2023).
- ✓ Kosinskaya E.V. The role of motivation in learning a foreign language // Territory of Science. 2015. No. 5. URL: https://cyberleninka.ru/article/n/rol-motivatsii-v-izuchenii-inostrannogo-yazyka-1 (date of access: 05/20/2023).
- ✓ Molkin Alexander Viktorovich MOTIVATION OF ADULTS IN THE SYSTEM OF ADDITIONAL EDUCATION // Lecturer XXI century. 2020.No.3-1. URL: https://cyberleninka.ru/article/n/motivatsiya-vzroslyh-v-sisteme-dopolnitelnogo-obrazovaniya (date of access: 05/20/2023).
- ✓ https://mel.fm/blog/yelizaveta-yermolenko/83690-pochemu-vzroslym-tyazhelo-uchitsya-i-kak-sebya-motivirovat
- ✓ https://skillbox.ru/media/education/kak-motivirovat-vzroslykh-uchitsya/
- ✓ https://www.unicraft.org/blog/5415/kak-obuchat-vzroslyh/

The War Prayer: Mark Twain's Powerful Critique of War and Blind Patriotism

Abstract:
This article examines in detail the personal and creative life of American writer Mark Twain. As well as his works about the war and harsh accusations against the war and, in particular, about blind patriotic and religious zeal as motives for the war.

Key words:
War, American literature, Civil War, relevance.

Introduction

One of the most significant moments in the history of American literature, the American Civil War (1861–1865) is still used as a dividing line in overview courses and reference works on American literature from the XIX century. Nonfictional genres including letters, diaries, and memoirs are frequently found in Civil War literature. Questions of how a nation's history is generated through collective memory and how it is portrayed in the culture of the time are of particular relevance. The sentiments of the time about race, gender, ethnicity, class, and the cause for war were also examined through the lens of Civil War literature. Along with historical inquiries regarding fiction created during the Civil War era, popular science texts' examination as literature resulted in important multidisciplinary research and posed helpful questions. At this time, many American writers were dominated by the theme of military operations.

Main part

Mark Twain (real name Samuel Langhorne Clemens) was born November 30, 1835 in Florida (Missouri, USA). On the day of his birth, Halley's comet flew over the Earth. An interesting fact is that on the day of the writer's death, the same comet will again sweep over the Earth. Mark Twain's father, John Marshall, worked as a judge, and his mother, Jane Lampton, was a housewife. However, despite the seemingly good position of the father, the family experienced serious financial difficulties. In this regard, the Clemens family decided to move to the shipping city of Hannibal. It was this small town with its sights that left many pleasant and warm memories in the memory of the future writer, playing an important role in Twain's biography11.

Childhood and youth. When Twain was 12 years old, his father died of pneumonia, leaving behind a lot of debt. For this reason, the children had to leave school and go to work. Soon, Twain's older brother began publishing a newspaper. As a result, Mark began to work in it as a compositor. It was then thatthe young man began to sometimes write his own articles. At the age of 18, Twain goes on a trip to the cities of America. During this period of his biography, he awakens a special interest in literature . He spends a lot of time in libraries, reading books of various genres. Over time, Mark Twain becomes a pilot on a ship. In his own words, he really liked this profession, which requires attention and knowledge of the fairway. However, when the civil war broke out in 1861, private shipping fell into decline. As a result, the guy had to look for another job.

---

11 History.com Editors. (2020). "Mark Twain is born." Retrieved December 5, 2022, from https://www.history.com/this-day-in-history/mark-twain-is-born

Creative biography of Twain. Over time, Mark Twain goes to the Wild West to mine precious metals. Despite the fact that the mines did not make him rich, during this period of his biography he managed to compose several witty stories. In 1863, the writer signs his books for the first time with the pseudonym Mark Twain, taken from shipping practice. In the future, he will publish all his works only under this name, and it is with him that he will go down in the history of world literature.The debut work in Twain's biography was The Famous Jumping Frog of Calaveras. This humorous story gained great popularity throughout America. After that, Twain began to actively engage in writing. He was offered to cooperate with many authoritative publications that wanted them to publish the works of a rising literary star. Soon, Mark discovers his gift as an orator, in connection with which he often begins to speak in different halls in front of a large audience. During this period of his biography, he meets his future wife Olivia, who was the sister of his friend. Twain's works. At the peak of his popularity, Mark Twain wrote several books in the realism genre, which received many positive reviews from critics.In 1876, the famous story "The Adventures of Tom Sawyer" came out from under his pen, which brought him even greater popularity. Interestingly, it contained many autobiographical episodes from the life of the author. After that, Mark Twain's new historical novel "The Prince and the Pauper" is published.Twain then published a fantasy novel, A Connecticut Yankee in King
Arthur's Court. The heroes of this work could travel in time. In the mid-1880s, Mark Twain opened his own publishing house, in which he printed the novel The Adventures of Huckleberry Finn. Later, he publishes the best-selling book Reminiscences, which he dedicates to U.S. President Ulysses S. Grant. Twain's

printing house lasted about 10 years until it completely went bankrupt due to the economic crisis that began in the United States12.

Death. In the last decade of his life, Mark Twain had to experience many tragedies associated with his family. He survived the death of three children and his wife Olivia, whom he loved very much. Perhaps that is why in this period of his biography he finally lost faith in God and began to promote atheism. This was especially noticeable in the works "The Mysterious Stranger" and "Letter from the Earth", published after the death of the classic.

Samuel Clemens, known to the world as Mark Twain, died on April 21, 1910 at the age of 74. The official cause of his death was angina pectoris. The writer was buried in the state of New York at Woodlawn Cemetery in Elmira.

Mark Twain "The War Prayer"

The War Prayer a short story or poem in prose by Mark Twain, which is a sharp accusation of war and, in particular, blind patriotic and religious zeal as motives for war.

It was a time of great excitement and uplift. The whole country was eager to fight - there was a war, the sacred fire of patriotism burned in the chest of each and every one; drums rumbled, bands played, toy pistols fired, clusters of rockets hissed and crackled into the air; wherever you look, along the roofs and balconies that are lost in the distance, a shaky thicket of flags sparkled in the sun; every day the young volunteers, cheerful and so beautiful in their new uniforms, marched along the wide avenue, and their fathers, mothers, sisters and brides

---

12 https://www.poemhunter.com/mark-twain/

greeted them with joyful voices on the way; every evening dense crowds of people listened with bated breath to some patriot orator whose speech touched the innermost strings of their souls, and now and then interrupted it with a storm of applause, while tears flowed down their cheeks; in the churches, the priests urged the people to faithfully serve the fatherland and so ardently and eloquently prayed to the god of war to send us help in a just cause, that among the listeners there would not be a single one who would not be moved to tears. It was indeed a glorious, wonderful time, and those few reckless men who dared to disapprove of the war and doubt its justice were immediately rebuked so severely and angry that, for their own safety, they thought it best to get out of sight and keep quiet13. Sunday came - the next day the troops went to the front; the church was filled to capacity in the morning, there were also volunteers, whose young faces burned in anticipation of military exploits; mentally they were already there - here they are advancing, stubbornly, faster and more decisively, a swift onslaught, a flash of sabers, the enemy is running, panic, powder smoke, furious pursuit, capitulation! - and here they are again at home: the heroes, hardened in battles, long-awaited and adored, returned from the war, in the golden glow of victory! Their loved ones sat next to the volunteers, proud and happy, arousing the envy of friends and neighbors who did not have brothers and sons whom they could send to the battlefield to win victory for their homeland or die a heroic death.The service went on as usual: the priest read the military chapter from the Old Testament, then the first prayer; the organ boomed, shaking the building;

---

13 https://www.americanyawp.com/reader/19-american-empire/mark-twain-the-war-prayer-ca-1904-5/

Lord, looking menacingly at the earth,
Lightnings, thunders are obedient to You!

Then followed a "long" prayer. No one could recall anything equal to her in the passion and penetration of feeling and in the beauty of presentation14. They asked in it most of all that our all-merciful and merciful Father would protect our valiant young soldiers, would be their help, support and support in their exploits in the name of the fatherland; that He would bless them and protect them in the day of battle and in the hour of danger, hold them in His right hand, give them strength and confidence, and make them invincible in bloody battles; so that He would help them crush the enemy, grant them, their weapons and country eternal honor and glory ... At that moment, an elderly stranger entered the church and slowly, silently, walked along the main aisle to the altar. His eyes were fixed on the priest, a tall figure was clothed in clothes that reached to the heels, and gray hair fell in a luxuriant mane over his shoulders, framing his wrinkled face, unnaturally, even deathly pale. Everyone looked at him in bewilderment, and he, silently walking between the pews, climbed onto the pulpit and stood expectantly next to the priest. Closing his eyelids and not suspecting the presence of a stranger, the priest continued to read his exciting prayer and ended it with a passionate call: “Bless our army, grant us victory, Lord our God, father and defender of our land and weapon!"

---

14 https://study.com/learn/lesson/the-war-prayer-mark-twain-summary-controversies-analysis.html

Conclusion

The discourse of American literature can still be explained by the changing political, social and cultural prerequisites that signaled the acceptance of Civil War in both countries. Academic and public debate in the United States since the 1960s. Usually we don't think that literature will change you, if so, we are looking for specific causes and effects. But literature often flows like a conversation during a Civil War – it awakens, gives a moment to act, rises to create the next parody, connects news events with established ones, appeals to both reason and emotions. We will not be able to understand how people survived the war if we look for it only in realistic descriptions and through later prisms of literary taste. Mark Twain, like other writers, made a huge contribution to the development of American literature.

References:

- History.com Editors. (2020). "Mark Twain is born." Retrieved December 5, 2022, from https://www.history.com/this-day-in-history/mark-twain-is-born
- https://www.poemhunter.com/mark-twain
- https://study.com/learn/lesson/the-war-prayer-mark-twain-summary-controversies-analysis.html
- https://www.americanyawp.com/reader/19-american-empire/mark-twain-the-war-prayer-ca-1904-5/

Expand Your Vocabulary: The Top 5 Books for Language Enrichment

Abstract:

The article touches upon the topic of studying vocabulary located on the periphery of the language and having a limited area of use. The article also discusses various methods by which you can expand your vocabulary.

Key words:

method, vocabulary, grammar, communication, lecicon, passive and active types of vocabulary

Lexicon is the establishment of language in a nutshell, lexicon is vital since it's the premise of all dialect. It's the crude building squares that we will utilize to precise our considerations and concepts, share data, get it others and develop individual connections. Even in the event that we scarcely know a dialect and have zero get a handle on of language structure, ready to still communicate (in spite of the fact that we might conclusion up sounding like cavemen!)15

Vocabulary Definition

Vocabulary is indicated as "the gather and collection of words that are known and utilized by a specific person". It can too be characterized as "a list or collection of words

---

15 Мирсалихова, Р.Т. Влияние лексики на улучшение рецептивных и продуктивных навыков / Р.Т. Мирсалихова. — Текст: электронный // NovaInfo, 2022. — № 131. — С. 108-110. — URL: https://novainfo.ru/article/19068 (дата обращения: 26.06.2022).

or expressions that are regularly in order organized and characterized or explained». Vocabulary is additionally commonly called word stock, lexis, and lexicon.

Importance of Vocabulary

Vocabulary is a basic portion of anyone's life and the taking after focuses portray the significance of vocabulary:

- vocabulary is basic for communication and expression.
- vocabulary shapes the premise of perusing comprehensi on
- Linguistic lexicon and considering lexicon work parallel
- Vocabulary too shapes a premise for judgment numerous times
- For passing on anything, lexicon is critical

One of the most important tasks in learning a foreign language is not only practice with grammar, but also the expansion of vocabulary. The more words you know, the more situations you will be able to explain yourself - even if you have big problems with articles and the formation of tenses, you are likely to be understood. And if you know few words, then nothing can be done about it. It is important to understand that there are two types of vocabulary - active and passive. The first of these consists of words that you actively use, and the second is vocabulary that you "know" and understand. There are ways to increase the vocabulary of both types.16

1. Read a lot (various texts)

16 https://habr.com/ru/post/471912/

It is one of the most obvious advices and the most effective ones. Reading allows students to get acquainted with a large number of words in what is probably the most effective context for their application. Often this allows to guess the meaning of the word, even if students do not know it - simply due to the words surrounding it. Teachers can recommend to their students to read anything, they can read books, histories, articles, magazines or newspapers. Reading is a great way to expand passive vocabulary.

2. Play word games

Scrabble, crosswords, Jeopardy - any game built around words will be useful for task. This is a great way to expand student's vocabulary, because it works as if "in the background", student does not learn anything separately, but memorize words during the game.

3. Use a dictionary

Of course, it is also a widely used method for improving vocabulary. Students can use dictionaries to memorize translations of some words, they can record not only the meaning of the word, but also the translation into their native language. This method is used in all educational institutions.

Reasons for Enhancing the Lexicon List of English Words

- Vocabulary advancement for reading comprehensions.

If you need to qualify for exams such as ACT, MCAT or SAT you would like to improve your dialect as these exams will test your capability in both English language structure and lexicon when reading comprehensions.

- Improving communication skills.

As mentioned before, making strides your communication abilities are required for various purposes. Apart from engaging in astute talks, you'll be able better express yourself as well as get it the person with whom you're communicating.

- Enhancement driving to way better individual, social and career life

Language improvement can assist you see the world better. During the method, you may get it not as it were the words, sentence structures or elocutions but too the concept of all these and how or why they are utilized. With legitimate preparing in a language enrichment course, you may too be able to clear numerous misguided judgments that you just had approximately a few words and their uses.

I display to your consideration the best 5 books for growing your vocabulary:

1. "McGraw-Hill Basic ESL Dictionary". The advantage of this lexicon is that it has been made particularly for the English dialect learner. This implies that the book has been outlined in a way that's simple to get it so that nothing gets misplaced in translation.
2. English Vocabulary in Use Series. One of the most delightful highlights of this arrangement is that understudies can select to consider American English or British English, which is extraordinary for people preparing for IELTS or TOEFL.
3. "504 Absolutely Basic Words" This lexicon book is best for individuals who need to memorize survival English or got to build a solid establishment some time recently moving on to more advanced material. Just like

the title recommends, it covers more than 500 of the foremost imperative and as often as possible used words in English.

4. "Word Power Made Easy" The lexicon words come with a number of clarifications that put definitions into setting, so you'll get distant better; a much better; a higher; a stronger; an improvement much better thought of how to appropriately utilize these words in discussion and writing.
5. "NTC Lexicon Builders". This book is outlined for progressed English learners who require help with English lexicon utilized in a proficient setting. This makes this arrangement of books culminate for understudies who are learning commerce English or ought to be a capable English speaker at work.17

---

17 htttps://www.fluentu.com/blog/english/english-vocabulary-books/

References:

1. https://habr.com/ru/post/471912/
2. https://internationalteacherstraining.com/blog/the-importance-and-methods-of-enriching-your-english-vocabulary
3. https://www.vedantu.com/commerce/vocabulary-and-types-of-vocabulary
4. htttps://www.fluentu.com/blog/english/english-vocabulary-books/
5. Мирсалихова, Р.Т. Влияние лексики на улучшение рецептивных и продуктивных навыков / Р.Т. Мирсалихова. — Текст: электронный // NovaInfo, 2022. — № 131. — С. 108-110. — URL: https://novainfo.ru/article/19068 (дата обращения: 26.06.2022).

Has social media made people more or less connected ?

Abstract:

Social networking websites enable us to interact, exchange information, participate in activities, events, play games, and listen to music, all of which contribute to the creation of our own virtual social spaces where we can distinguish ourselves from other people. Although many of us love using social media to remain in touch, excessive use can lead to addiction, anxiety, melancholy, loneliness, and FOMO. Therefore, the current study is focused on how social networks have increased or decreased human connectivity.

Key words:

social media, connection, Internet, network, social isolation

One of the Internet's most popular resources at the moment is social networking. They are utilized by approximately 85% of all Internet users worldwide, according to the research company comScore. A number of scientists contend that continuity, mass character, and quality are the three most significant fundamental issues facing the contemporary educational paradigm (Voronkin, 2014).

A social network is a community of people who share common interests, a cause, or other reasons for communicating directly with one another. A social network is defined by the general philosophical approach as a collection of social objects and their relationships (Patarakin & Shustov, 2013).

The influence of social networks on a person and his life is enormous, many do not even fully realize the scale of this phenomenon, and social networks are already the most popular activity on the Internet. Today, out of the 100 most visited sites in the world, 20 are classic social networks and another 60 are socialized to some extent. More than 80% of companies around the world use social networks in their work. About 78% of people trust information from social networks. Entire revolutions are even organized through them. Social networks have become the very center of the modern Internet. About 3.5 billion people use social media, and more than 1 million people open a social media account every day. Individuals with access to digital devices spend nearly 2.5 hours on social media every day (Regis College, 2021).

With an ever-increasing number of people using social media on a daily basis, there is no doubt that social media offer a variety of advantages that span all facets of life. In terms of human connection, students for specifics, adolescents can instantly connect with family, friends, and even strangers beyond face-to-face distance and share their lives via photos, videos, or even text status updates (Anderson & Jiang, 2018). These connections can help with a variety of things, like getting advice from others, looking for a new job, finding help, making free ads, and so on (Express News Service, 2015). The use of social media to strengthen existing relationships or create new meaningful connections is the most effective way to combat loneliness. However, if it is used in place of actual social interaction, it is counterproductive (Patulny, 2020).

Social Media Contributes to Social Isolation

In 1998, just as a lot of people started using the internet, the first study that looked into this phenomenon was published. The researchers observed 169 individuals over the first two years of their internet use to see whether this new medium made them more or less social. They discovered that: "...more Internet use was connected with participants' decreased communication with family members in the household, decreased social circle size, and increased melancholy and loneliness" (Kraut et.al., 1998). This was seen as quite the paradox, given that the individuals were using the internet extensively as a communication technology.

A 2004 study comparing online engagement with face-to-face interaction came to the same conclusion: "Despite its extensive use as a communication tool, the Internet has been associated to poorer levels of social well-being" (Moody, 2004).

A 2014 study on college students with internet addiction revealed the following ten years later: "The results show that long-term, harmful, and excessive Internet use would cause feelings of loneliness to increase...[.] This study also found that social interactions with family members online were ineffective at reducing depressive symptoms when compared to unconnected social relationships " (Yao et.al., 2014).

The use of social media in ways that connect with others makes you feel less lonely and social. Unfortunately, as our social media usage increases, we become more and more lonely. This trend suggests that we may not be using social media in the most social way and comparing ourselves to others. The convenience of interaction may come at the expense of face-to-face interaction. Both increase the likelihood of social isolation.

References

Anderson , M., & Jiang, J. (2018). *Teens and their experiences on social media.* Pew Research Center: Internet, Science & Tech. Retrieved December 20, 2022, from https://www.pewresearch.org/internet/2018/11/28/teens-and-their-experiences

Express News Service (2015). *Social media sites help to connect to people worldwide.* The Indian Express. Retrieved December 20, 2022, from https://indianexpress.com/article/cities/mumbai/social-media-sites-help-to-connect-to-people-worldwide/

Kraut, R., Patterson, M., Lundmark, V., Kiesler, S., Mukophadhyay, T., & Scherlis, W. (1998). *Internet paradox: A social technology that reduces social involvement and psychological well-being?* American Psychologist, 53(9), 1017–1031. https://doi.org/10.1037/0003-066X.53.9.1017

Moody, E. (2004). *Internet use and its relationship to loneliness.* CyberPsychology & Behavior. Retrieved December 20, 2022, from https://www.liebertpub.com/doi/10.1089/109493101300210303

Patarakin, E., & Shustov, S. (2013). *Digital Ecology: Social Networks and informational ecosystems.* Vestnik of Minin University. Retrieved December 20, 2022, from https://www.minin-vestnik.ru/jour/article/view/424?locale=en_US

Regis College(2021). *Does social media create isolation?* Retrieved December 20, 2022, from https://online.regiscollege.edu/blog/does-social-media-create-isolation/

University of Wollongong (2020). *Does social media make us more or less lonely? Depends on how you use it* . UOW. Retrieved December 20, 2022, from https://www.uow.edu.au/media/2020/does-social-media-make-us-more-or-less-lonely-depends-on-how-you-use-it.php

Voronkin, A. S. (2014). *Social networks: evolution, structure, analysis.* Educational Technology and Society, 17(1), 650-675.

Yao, M., & Zhi-jin, Z. (2014). *Loneliness, Social Contacts and Internet Addiction: A Cross-Lagged Panel Study.* Computers in Human Behavior. Retrieved December 20, 2022, from https://doi.org/10.1016/j.chb.2013.08.007

Influence of the First Language on Second Language Learning: Exploring the Interplay between L1 and L2

Abstract:
This article is dedicated to the influence of the L1 on learning L2. The process of studying foreign language speech is inextricably linked with the problem of the interaction of two language systems in the speaker's mind. The use of the native language should be conscious and purposeful and be limited to a certain number of situations where it not only does not interfere, but also contributes to the optimization of the educational process.

Key words:
L1, L2, influence, language learning, acquisition, interference

Introduction

The importance of foreign languages around the world has been proven repeatedly. Language education plays a leading role in the development of the personality, since it is a tool for creating and interpreting the "image of the world", penetrating into the world culture and realizing one's national and cultural affiliation, forming and socializing the personality.

Anton Pavlovich Chekhov, the great Russian writer, classic, said: "How many languages you know - so many times you are a person." In the modern world, when business, scientific and cultural contacts are developing and strengthening, when relations with other countries are becoming closer, knowledge of foreign languages plays an important role. Knowledge of several foreign languages becomes a necessity. At present, a modern person must know foreign languages well, because mutual understanding between peoples is of great importance for peaceful cooperation.

The study of languages has become such a topical issue in the life of every nation that Goethe said in this regard "who does not know a single foreign language does not know his own".

Literature Review

L1 is the speaker's first language, and L2 is the second language. Everyone knows that we learn our native language by acquisition (assimilation). This means that we don't need to learn grammar or vocabulary to speak it. Language acquisition is the process by which people acquire the ability to perceive and comprehend language (in other words, acquire the ability to be aware of language and understand it), as well as create and use words and sentences for communication[18].

But before learning a second language (L2), you should learn its grammar and vocabulary to communicate with others. This is called language learning. Language learning is the process of actively trying to learn and understand a language. Language learning occurs more consciously and is most likely the result of formal teaching. Perhaps similar to how a second language is learned[19].

18https://encyclopedia.pub
19 https://beelinguapp.com

The most significant impact of the native or, rather, the first language on the second, lies in the fact that a student who is beginning to learn a second language attempts to incorporate and apply these norms in relation to the new language. This attempt may be made consciously or unconsciously (at school or in earlier years) if the student is aware of the norms and rules of the grammar of his native language. Before the age of twelve or thirteen, a youngster who begins learning a foreign language typically speaks it without an accent. Yet, those who started learning a new language after the age of eighteen typically struggle to overcome the structure and phonetic influence of their native language. The difficulty of overcoming the linguistic interference of one's original language increases with age, and doing so needs the person's intentional efforts. A youngster automatically starts studying the culture of his environment, which shapes his identity, as soon as he starts learning his native language, which is the language of his environment. As a result, a person's acquired cultural and personal traits last until the end of their lives. An adult thus develops a new identity through learning a foreign language, and it is challenging for him to lose the identity that is based on his mother tongue. The second emerging identity causes the linguistic essence, the foundation of each person's individuality, to feel endangered. Because of this, a youngster is better able to resist the challenges of learning a second language than an adult because of their more malleable character and thinking20.

---

20 Vokhmyakova Elena Sergeevna (2019). The influence of the native language on the process of learning a foreign language. Problems of modern teacher education, (63-1), 70-73.

The issue of the original tongue's influence on language learning is one that never goes away. If the student's language proficiency is lower and there isn't enough time set out for practical sessions, this influence will be stronger. Unquestionably of relevance to both the theory and practice of teaching is the study of the issue of the impact of the native language on the process of teaching a foreign language. The ratio of the two languages—the native and foreign—must be considered in this situation. The outcome, or efficacy of the methodological procedures employed, depends not only on the trainees' basic level and learning capacity, but also on the standard of the learning process itself. Working alone can result in a haphazard blending of two languages, particularly if they are closely related. Also, the learning process does not have the right effect on the development of communication skills and capacities if the trainees lack long-term drive. When learning a foreign language, it's important to compare the phonetic, lexical, and grammatical structures of the studied and native languages to create a communication unit.

First language acquisition

First language acquisition should not be overlooked because it can help learners become more proficient in their chosen language. Although L2 usage is encouraged, L1 usage should be permitted when necessary when learning a foreign language[21]. Although the mother language is not a good foundation for a technique, Atkinson contends that it has a variety of responsibilities to perform at all levels that are

21 Weschler, R. (1997). Uses of Japanese (L1) in English Classroom: Introducing the FunctionalTranslation Method, The Internet TESL Journal.

currently constantly underestimated22. L1 is a helpful tool for learners to use as they advance in their language proficiency. A complete restriction on L1 use will make it more difficult for learners to understand the target language. "Don't forbid mother tongue use but encourage attempts to utilize the target language," advises Willis23.

Interlingual interference is the term used to describe how a native language negatively affects a foreign language when being taught. Interlingual interference can appear at any linguistic level, including the phonetic, lexical, and grammatical. As a result, there is grammatical, lexical, and phonetic interlingual interference24. Interlingual errors are often referred to as language transfer or interlingual interference. It is characterized as the outcome of language transfer, which is brought on by the learner's mother tongue.

In their second language (L2), many speakers have an accent that is shaped by their first language (L1) and is therefore perceived as non-native-like. It is less well attested if and under what conditions prolonged exposure to an L2 influences the way one pronounces L1 speech sounds.

The main functions of the native language in a foreign language lesson:

---

22 Atkinson, D. (1987). The mother tongue in the classroom: A neglected resource? ELT Journal, 44(4), 241-247

23 Willis, J. (1996). A framework for task-based learning. Harlow: Longman.

24 Samarskaya S.V. (2017). The influence of interlingual grammatical transference and interference on the study of a foreign language. Actual problems of philology and pedagogical linguistics, (3 (27)), 210-216.

1. Motivational function. The native language is often used in the formulation of the lesson, in the introduction of the teacher in order to arouse the interest of students in the upcoming work.

2. Use of the native language when debriefing at the end of the lesson. This is a very important element of learning communication, and the educator should verbalize what the students have learned in the session to provide a sense of progress.

3. Creation by the teacher of a problem situation in the lesson. The teacher motivates the subsequent introduction of speech and language material, as well as the formulation of creative tasks, an explanation of their preparation and design.

4. Many teachers turn to mother tongue at the stage of presentation of grammatical material.

5. The native language is used by the teacher when explaining the material of a linguistic and cultural nature. This allows to remove the difficulties in understanding the peculiarities of thinking and worldview of representatives of another culture25.

Conclusion

When learning a new language, the native language is crucial. The importance of intercultural conversation in today's globalized society has caused us to reassess how we view foreign-speaking nations and their linguistic peculiarities. In the process of learning a foreign language, the student develops his own autonomous language system that combines the key

---

25 Erokhina E.A. (2017). The meaning and role of the native language in teaching a foreign language. Actual problems of the humanities and natural sciences, (9-2), 58-62.

elements of both his native tongue and the non-native language being studied, i.e., a foreign language, by drawing on his native tongue. The student is making steady progress in mastering the structure of a non-native language by drawing on his native linguocultural background.

References:

1. Atkinson, D. (1987). The mother tongue in the classroom: A neglected resource? ELT Journal, 44(4), 241-247
2. Erokhina E.A. (2017). The meaning and role of the native language in teaching a foreign language. Actual problems of the humanities and natural sciences, (9-2), 58-62.
3. Samarskaya S.V. (2017). The influence of interlingual grammatical transference and interference on the study of a foreign language. Actual problems of philology and pedagogical linguistics, (3 (27)), 210-216.
4. Vokhmyakova Elena Sergeevna (2019). The influence of the native language on the process of learning a foreign language. Problems of modern teacher education, (63-1), 70-73.
5. Weschler, R. (1997). Uses of Japanese (L1) in English Classroom: Introducing the FunctionalTranslation Method, The Internet TESL Journal.
6. Willis, J. (1996). A framework for task-based learning. Harlow: Longman.
7. https://beelinguapp.com/blog/language-learning-versus-learning-acquisition#:~:text=Language%20learning%20(LL)%20is%20the,of%20gaining%20language%20knowledge%20naturally
8. https://encyclopedia.pub/entry/35237#:~:text=Language%20acquisition%20is%20the%20process,words%20and%20sentences%20to%20communicate
   https://encyclopedia.pub/entry/35237#:~:text=Language%20acquisition%20is%20the%20process,words%20and%20sentences%20to%20communicate

The Importance of Transferable Skills: Enhancing Leadership, Teamwork, and Problem-Solving in Education

Abstract:

In this article, the author shows the importance of using transferable skills to improve the quality of education.

Key words:

transferable skills, leadership, educational process, communication, teamwork, problem solving skills.

Introduction

Technological improvements let people to open new skills. Individuals improve their skills in order to get a well-paid job or study abroad. And I am sure that one of the most essential skills are transferable skills. Transferable skills include skills such as problem solving, analytical reasoning, critical thinking, leadership, teamwork, communication.

Literature Review

Transferable skills are universally essential for every branch. They contribute to success and the victory of a group, client, or organization. They are important in studying, job and other branch0es that any personnel come across in their lifestyle. In addition to this, they permit to control over a career way and guarantee an advancement in career change. In a way, these are abilities that never go out of style. Transferable skills will take after and back your victory professionally, so long as you contribute and put deliberateness exertion into sharpening them.

The most important transferable skills that we use in educational process:

- Critical thinking. What is meant by critical thinking? Critical thinking is the type of thinking that helps to be critical of any statements, not to take anything for granted without evidence, but at the same time be open to new ideas and methods. Critical thinking is a necessary condition for freedom of choice, quality of forecast, responsibility for one's own decisions. Critical thinking, therefore, is essentially a kind of tautology, a synonym for qualitative thinking. It is rather a name than a concept, but it is under this name that, with a number of international projects, the technological methods that we will present below came into our lives. The constructive basis of the "technology of critical thinking" is the basic model of three stages of the organization of the educational process: At the stage of recall from memory, the existing knowledge and ideas about what is being studied are "called", actualized, personal interest is formed, the goals of considering a particular topic are determined. At the stage of comprehension (or realization of meaning), as a rule, the student comes into contact with new information. It is being systematized. The student gets the opportunity to think about the nature of the object being studied, learns to formulate questions as he correlates old and new information. There is a formation of one's own position. It is very important that already at this stage, using a number of techniques, it is already possible to independently monitor the process of understanding the material. The stage of reflection (reflection) is characterized by the fact that students consolidate new knowledge and actively rebuild their own primary ideas in order to include new concepts in them. 26

- Leadership. Leadership competence is defined by us as the ability and readiness to solve leadership problems: vision of the goal, motivation of oneself and others to achieve it, organization of activities to achieve it. In education, there are at least three aspects of leadership. The first is the education of leaders as the goal of the educational process in organizations; the second - leadership as a principle of management of the leaders of these organizations; the third is the leadership of the educational organizations themselves in the market of educational services27.
- Communication. By educational communication we mean the process of intellectual and emotional exchange of information, during which information is collected, redistributed and interpersonal contacts are established — the teacher and the student in the classroom28. In the technological era, various applied communication methods are used, which

---

26https://kpmuk1.edu.yar.ru/metodicheskie_rekomendatsii/sovremennie_pedagogicheskie_tehnologii.html?with_template=blind

27Savina Natalya Viktorovna Leadership in education // European research. 2016. No. 8 (19). URL: https://cyberleninka.ru/article/n/liderstvo-v-obrazovanii (date of access: 08/11/2022).

28 Висторобская, В. Д. К вопросу об учебной коммуникации в педагогическом взаимодействии участников образовательного процесса / В. Д. Висторобская. — Текст : непосредственный // Молодой ученый. — 2017. — № 15 (149). — С. 556-560. — URL: https://moluch.ru/archive/149/42061/ (дата обращения: 11.08.2022).

are additional methods in the educational process. There is always some way of communication between a teacher and a student. A student can feel confident only when the teacher trusts his student 100%. He, that is, the student, should always feel the support of the teacher. As a young teacher, I realized that students first of all need motivation and trust.

- Teamwork. In order to develop students' leadership skills, it is necessary to conduct group classes. Here we see a close connection between teamwork and leadership. A Chinese proverb answers this question very eloquently: "Behind one capable person there are always other capable people." Teamwork is a combination of personal qualities and professional skills of several people. With such an arsenal, where the beneficial sides of the team can be freely juggled, the highest results can be achieved. That is why effective interaction only strengthens its positions. I am sure that the work of the team improves the quality of perception and analysis of information. I can give you an example, in a language camp, an educational game was held between the participants, in which the main goal was to show the advantages of teamwork. The participants were given the task to number the necessary things that they would need on the moon. After that, we collected all the sheets and divided them into teams. The trainer re-distributed new sheets on which the participants worked in mini-groups. The results were unexpected, as it was found that most of the participants work in teamwork much more effectively than in individual work. I think that teachers should conduct more such educational and logical games. Because in the future, the student will have to work in a team and find a common language with everyone.

- Problem-solving. Albert Einstein formulated an idea: "The formulation of a problem is much more important than its solution, which may be just a matter of mathematical or experimental skills". Problem solving skills are a major part in the learning process. Especially such sciences as mathematics or physics require a special approach to solving the problem.

References:

- https://abakus-center.ru/blog/310-rabota-v-komande-zachem-uchit-detej-effektivnomu-vzaimodejstviyu
- https://kpmuk1.edu.yar.ru/metodicheskie_rekomendatsii/sovremennie_pedagogicheskie_tehnologii.html?with_template=blind
- Savina Natalya Viktorovna Leadership in education // European research. 2016. No. 8 (19). URL: https://cyberleninka.ru/article/n/liderstvo-v-obrazovanii (date of access: 08/11/2022).
- Висторобская, В. Д. К вопросу об учебной коммуникации в педагогическом взаимодействии участников образовательного процесса / В. Д. Висторобская. — Текст : непосредственный // Молодой ученый. — 2017. — № 15 (149). — С. 556-560. — URL: https://moluch.ru/archive/149/42061/ (дата обращения: 11.08.2022).

Expanding Language Learning Opportunities: Harnessing the Power of the Internet and ICT

Abstract:

This article examines the concept of online resources in learning English, and the article also recommends useful sites for students and teachers.

Key words:

Internet, online resources, education, communication, e-books, ICT.

Introduction

In the modern world, scientists have made many inventions to make life easier and improve the quality of life. These are all kinds of household appliances, various equipment, computers, the Internet. The Internet can rightly be called one of the best inventions, as it is currently used by almost every person.

The Internet has intruded very tightly into human life. A person uses the Internet in various spheres of his life. And one of these areas is the field of education. It can be rightfully assumed that in modern society education is closely connected with social networks, especially it was clearly noticeable when education in educational institutions was conducted in a distance format. Learning a second language is one of the most important areas in the modern world. Young people actively use Internet resources to learn foreign languages.

Literature review

Internet sources can be used for various educational purposes. The global Internet creates the conditions for obtaining any information necessary for students and teachers. In addition, students can take part in various competitions and olympiads held on the Internet. It is important to note that now it has become possible to participate in these events not only at the state level, but also at the global level.

To the Internet information resources used in the learning process, these include:

- databases, information systems, reference files, dictionaries, reference books;
- training systems, courses, programs for self-education;
- educational video and audio recordings;
- electronic libraries (newspapers, magazines, books in electronic form);
- distance learning courses;
- email, etc.

The main advantages for students of using the Internet in the educational

process include:

1. improving computer literacy (improving the skills of handling and working with a computer and the Internet);
2. development and improvement of skills of independent search for necessary information and work with it, as well as training and research;
3. formation of practical skills.

On the Internet you can find many resources that will help you learn the language. And you can also take online tests to determine the level of language proficiency, try yourself on preliminary international exams (mock tests), such as SAT, IELTS or TOEFL.

In foreign language education, great importance is given to communication, interactivity and autonomy of learning, and, importantly, to learning the language in the context of culture. The formation of intercultural competence is impossible without communication in the target language, and IT helps to simulate learning situations or implement theoretical skills in a real act of foreign language communication, including with the participation of native speakers of the target language.

Online tests, games and dictionaries can be found on various sites that offer both ready-made thematic developments and services for creating your own materials.

Research Methodology

Currently, many well-known publishing houses produce books not only in paper, but also in electronic format. I would especially like to note that currently one of the most popular languages in the world is English, this language is certainly called the language of business and travel.

I would like to suggest several sites that will help new students in learning English:

1.Englex.ru

All materials on the site of the Inglex online school are prepared by experienced English teachers who know how to work with elementary students.

2.Study.ru

Study.ru is a whole knowledge base for those who are just starting to learn English. The site has a guide to English grammar, structured phrasebooks for all situations, tests and other useful information for beginners.

3.Bistroenglish.com

Bistro English is a great site for those who want to learn modern spoken English in a simple, fun and freeway. Here you will find a rich collection of English lessons for beginners. You will study grammar, words and phrases for every day, phrasebooks for tourists, and also learn the language from films and songs. If you practice regularly, the results will not be long in coming.

4.Duolingo.com

Another Russian-language universal online resource for learning English for beginners is Duolingo. On this site, you can also practice English online for free, but you will not be accompanied by a lion cub, but by a funny green owl. On Duolingo, you learn words in context, in short, simple sentences. This is very convenient, since you can immediately use ready-made phrases in your speech.

In addition, for students who want to take the exam, I recommend sites that are free and useful for them. They can study independently and pass this international exam. These sites provide an opportunity to prepare for IELTS for free from scratch on your own or to supplement the main classes in the courses in this way. They usually cover all parts of IELTS (Listening, Reading, Writing and Speaking), include helpful articles, sample assignments, skills training resources and IELTS mock exams.

- ✓ GlobalExam

This is a universal international portal, the purpose of which is to help students prepare for various exams, including TOEFL,

DELF, TOEIC and many others. An impressive section of the site is devoted to preparing for the IELTS test. Here you will find useful tips and life hacks for preparing for the exam, manuals for learning English, IELTS practice tasks and interesting articles about the test and English in general.

- ✓ IELTS Exam

On this popular portal, you will find everything you need to know about the IELTS exam. Test descriptions, tasks, grammar, preparation tips and examples are a very useful resource from an informative point of view.

- ✓ IELTS Portal

The site of the IELTS preparation school will be useful not only for those who want to study at the school itself, but also for those who prepare for the exam on their own. There is a detailed description of all parts of the test, as well as resources for preparing for them - examples of tasks and answers, useful articles and much more. All this is in Russian, so this portal is especially convenient for Russian-speaking users.

- ✓ Polyu

Polyu is a very user friendly and easy to use IELTS preparation website. All site resources are sorted into four main sections: description, preparation tips and IELTS tests for self-examination and practice.

In addition, each section is provided with additional links, which can be especially helpful if you are preparing for IELTS on your own.

- ✓ EngVid

This site has hundreds of free videos to help you improve your English vocabulary and grammar quickly. Users can also

access videos on particularly difficult topics, such as idioms and differences between accents.
This is an excellent resource for those who are preparing for IELTS, primarily for preparing for the oral part of the exam.

- ✓ Examenglish

A detailed description of the test and answers to frequently asked questions can also be found on the Examenglish portal. The site contains practical tasks for all parts of the IELTS exam and a dictionary, sections with useful literature, links to applications and other useful resources.

- ✓ IELTS Blog

This is a simple and clear site that gives a complete picture of ILETS, structure, features and tasks of the exam. Here you can find tips for passing each part and each type of IELTS questions, as well as real examples of the tasks themselves, answers and essays for the written part of the exam

Conclusion

As I mentioned before, the Internet is an integral part of our life. Thus, without the use of ICT in the educational process, it is difficult to imagine modern lessons. ICT contributes to the activation of students' cognitive activity, increases interest in the study of specific academic disciplines, students have the opportunity to master the content of subjects in a bright, interesting way, as well as test their skills in interactive activities.

References:

- https://www.hotcourses.ru/study-abroad-info/subject-guides/free-online-sites-to-prepare-for-ielts/
- Костюченко М.В., Трутнев А.Ю. ИНТЕРНЕТ-РЕСУРСЫ ПРИ ИЗУЧЕНИИ АНГЛИЙСКОГО ЯЗЫКА // Международный журнал прикладных и фундаментальных исследований. – 2018. – № 1. – С. 181-185; URL: https://applied-research.ru/ru/article/view?id=12090 (дата обращения: 01.07.2022).
- Курбаниязов Б.В., Сидоров С.В. Возможности интернет-ресурсов при обучении иностранному языку [Электронный ресурс] // Сидоров С.В. Сайт педагога-исследователя – URL: http://si-sv.com/publ/vozmozhnosti_internet_resursov/6-1-0-657 (дата обращения: 01.07.2022).

Expanding Opportunities and Enhancing Language Learning: The Role of Innovative Methods and Information and Communication Technologies in Foreign Language Teaching

Annotation:

Teaching a foreign language is one of the most difficult tasks. Many teachers still use the old teaching methods, but the use of innovative methods in educational institutions expands the opportunities of students. Innovative technologies contribute to the development of the country's human potential.

Key words:

ICT, technology, methods, web-classes, information and communication technologies.

Introduction

At present, such alternative approaches, such as the development of communication, technical skills, interpersonal skills, ICT literacy, are becoming increasingly important. The need for successful graduates who are able to compete in the tough survival environment of the global market is very much in demand today. Nowadays the introduction of information and communication technologies (ICT) and interactive methods in the learning process is a priority in the methodology of teaching foreign languages. ICTs make it possible to involve pupils and students in dialogue, increase their interest in learning, enrich the educational process with various latest teaching methods, develop students' communicative competence and linguistic and cultural knowledge.

Literature review

Computer training programs have a number of advantages over traditional teaching methods, being, first of all, means of direct audiovisual interactive interaction. Using them in the classroom in combination with traditional teaching methods allows you to train various types of speech activity, realize the nature of linguistic phenomena, form linguistic abilities, create communicative situations, automate language and speech skills and ensure the implementation of an individual approach and the intensification of independent work of the student, as well as contributes to the increase of cognitive activity, motivation and the quality of students' knowledge.

Research methodology

Web-based learning is one of the fastest growing areas. Web classes are remote lessons, conferences, seminars, business games, laboratory work, workshops and other forms of training sessions conducted using telecommunications and other Internet capabilities. There are many different web classes for learning a foreign language.

In addition, with the development of technology, various free online courses appear.

Let's consider learning a foreign language using the example of English. English is one of the international languages that is used almost all over the world.

A modern teacher should use the following methods to effectively learn English:

o **The use of information and communication technologies.** The use of ICT at various stages of the lesson allows you to optimize the educational process, effectively use time. When explaining the new material for clarity, I use computer presentations in Microsoft Power Point (including those created by the students themselves, after a preliminary check by the teacher), videos from the site www.Youtube.com, educational films, video clips, excerpts from animated films.

o **Using the technology of project training and research activities.** I consider the project method to be one of the leading ones in the formation of students' speech competencies, the ability to use a foreign language as an instrument of intercultural communication and interaction. They talk to their comrades, firstly, they become more open, and secondly, they use their knowledge and skills in English in new non-standard situations.

o **Games.** Games allow for a differentiated approach to students, to involve each person in the work, taking into account his interests, aptitude, level of training in the language. Exercises of a playful nature enrich students with new impressions, activate vocabulary, perform a developmental function, relieve fatigue.

Information and communication technologies are a powerful means of teaching, monitoring and managing the educational process, as it is the most important parameter of the modern socio-cultural system. Internet resources are a familiar and convenient means of getting acquainted with the culture of other countries and peoples, communication, obtaining information, an inexhaustible source of the educational process. That is why a systematic approach to the reform of foreign language teaching methods using new information technologies is based on the concept of an information and learning environment, which is considered in close connection with the system of developing learning. The information and learning environment is a set of conditions that not only allow you to form and develop language knowledge, skills and abilities, but also contribute to the development of the student's personality.

Conclusion

ICT contributes to the activation of students' cognitive activity, increases interest in the study of specific academic disciplines, students have the opportunity to master the content of subjects in a bright, interesting way, as well as test their skills in interactive activities. But in order to learn any foreign language, a person must have a specific goal.

References:

- Mukhiddinova Sabokhat Akhmadzhanovna Modern approach to teaching foreign languages // Science, education and culture. 2016. No. 6 (9). URL: https://cyberleninka.ru/article/n/sovremennyy-podhod-k-obucheniyu-inostrannym-yazykam (date of access: 09/22/2022).
- Синовац Марина Анатольевна СОВРЕМЕННЫЕ ПОДХОДЫ И МЕТОДЫ В ОБУЧЕНИИ АНГЛИЙСКОМУ ЯЗЫКУ // Интерактивная наука. 2020. №7 (53). URL: https://cyberleninka.ru/article/n/sovremennye-podhody-i-metody-v-obuchenii-angliyskomu-yazyku (дата обращения: 22.09.2022).
- Kengessova A. USING OF MULTIMEDIA TECHNOLOGIES AT ENGLISH LESSONS ON THE

UPDATED EDUCATIONAL PROGRAM // Научное сообщество студентов: МЕЖДИСЦИПЛИНАРНЫЕ ИССЛЕДОВАНИЯ: сб. ст. по мат. CXVII междунар. студ. науч.-практ. конф. № 10(117). URL: https://sibac.info/archive/meghdis/10(117).pdf (д ата обращения: 10.09.2022)

- https://sberuniversity.ru/edutech
- https://pedsovet.org/article/sovremennye-obrazovatelnye-tehnologii-na-urokah-angliyskogo-yazyka-1
- Палагутина, М. А. Инновационные технологии обучения иностранным языкам / М. А. Палагутина, И. С. Серповская. — Текст: непосредственный // Проблемы и перспективы развития образования: материалы I Междунар. науч. конф. (г. Пермь, апрель 2011 г.). — Т. 1. — Пермь: Меркурий, 2011. — С. 156-159. — URL: https://moluch.ru/conf/ped/archive/17/578/ (дата обращения: 23.09.2022).
- Умаркулова, Д.С. Онлайн-ресурсы при изучении английского языка / Д.С. Умаркулова. — Текст: электронный // NovaInfo, 2022. — № 133. — С. 55-56. — URL: https://novainfo.ru/article/19323 (дата обращения: 23.09.2022).

The Importance of Effective Goal Setting and Planning for Achieving Success

Abstract:
In the article, the author examines the concept of goal-setting and goals. It discusses the issues of goal setting, what should be the final result of the goal, the influence of motivation on goal setting.

Key words:
motivation, goal, method, objective, self-determination

The formulation of goals, the issues of goal setting and goal formation are directly related to any branch of knowledge that studies and describes the conscious activity and behavior of a person (or other organic system). As a general scientific category, the goal is characterized as an idea of the state to which the given system aspires and for the sake of which exists, the definition of the goal as the anticipation in thinking of the result of the activity and the way of its organization with the help of certain means that has the same meaning. The goal integrates various human actions into some sequence or system.29

---

29 Хайруллаева, Д.С. Психологическо-дидактические свойства читательской компетенции в подготовке учителя иностранного языка / Д.С. Хайруллаева. — Текст: электронный // NovaInfo, 2022. — № 131. — URL: https://novainfo.ru/article/19051 (дата обращения: 06.04.2022)

A goal is a clear understanding of the desired result. A correctly set goal sets the criteria for its identification, that is, it makes it possible to reasonably answer the question - has the goal been achieved or not.

Each individual has their claim lifestyle. Models of behavior are customarily separated into two expansive bunches: versatile and goal-oriented. To begin with incorporates individuals who adjust to the conditions of life, the moment – those who are solidly moving towards the planning goal. Both models have their possess merits and demerits. Focusing on the cons, you will decide what to choose. Consider both sides of the coin in each of the ways.

Versatile people tend to go with stream, comply present day realities. Such individuals do not attempt to profoundly alter or move forward something. By nature, they are as rule kind and considering, esteem steadiness and perplexed of misfortunes due to a few changes in their lives. At the smallest trouble, opportunists tend to urge discouraged or have strongly anxiety. They do not make conditions, but get utilized to existing ones, attempting to unequivocally comply with certain standards and rules.

Purposeful individuals construct life themselves and do not go with the flow. Usually they are business people, high-class masters and fruitful individuals with shrewdness and experience. With solid character, pioneers are committed to achieving results and do not complain about the issues that arise. They tend to make for the purpose of greatest comfort.

Beneath the objective, each individual gets it something of his own:

- desired result of events;
- specific result of process;
- the anticipated adaptation of long run.

The objective ought to be clear and specific. Otherwise, it gets to be troublesome to achieve. Fuzzy goal-setting makes the premise for questions approximately the have to be total the task. Initial wants are overlooked; other needs emerge in their place.

Goal-setting could be a complex and rather long process. The fundamental trouble lies within the fundamental change characterized states of mind, within the creation of a natty gritty arrange for their usage and the choice of goals. In the course of the execution of the sketched out focuses of the arrange, blunders unavoidably emerge that have to redressed in a convenient manner.

The target can be everything that the person needs to attain, what he needs to realize. As a result, it is not continuously achievable. It may be an item of ponder action, volitional qualities and motivation. As within the case of inside mental forms, the concept of an objective can be anticipated onto the outside world.

The goal is idealized encapsulation of the result of any action and the ways to realize it with the assistance of particular tools. It is closely associated with the wants and eagerly of an individual, with his thought of a perfect future, with the will of the person and awareness. The properties of objectives (rightness, shared consistency, versatility and profundity) depend on the nature of the arrangement and changeability of the personality. Depth areas the level of impact of the target on different regions of life. This property characterizes the assignments of the key plan. Consistency may be a property that appears the relationship of a given objective with others, their shared influence. Plasticity is the property of changing over time. Due to slow arrangement of values, the objectives of the worldwide viral level moreover tend to transform. Correctness demonstrates the level of consistency of the settings of the strategic and vital arrange.

It ought to be recalled that it is not as it were a precisely formulated objective that's imperative, but moreover an accurate representation of the ways to realize it. Tools and assets must be clearly distinguished to assist accomplish the expecting result within the distributed time frame. This is encouraged by an extraordinarily created Savvy goal-setting innovation, within the truncation of which five quality criteria:

4. **Specific:** The most specific goal that indicates a specific outcome.
5. **Measurable:** The goal must lead to a measurable result, either quantitatively or qualitatively. In the first case, the figure that needs to be achieved is fixed. In the second, a standard is given.
6. **Achievable:** the goal must be achievable, and the results and methods real.
7. **Relevant:** the relevance of achieving the goal at the time of reaching the result is necessary.
8. **Time-bound:** the goal must be urgent, that is, clearly limited in time to reach.

Brian Tracy's Method. On a chunk of paper, you would like to compose 10 objectives for the another year in such a way, on the off chance that they had already been implemented. For case, "I gone to 10 states in 10 weeks". Choose the foremost critical one that can alter your life from the composed "realized" goals. Fix it, copy it on the moment sheet of paper and work it out agreeing to the SMART method.

In order to achieve this goal, you must include strong, confident, factual evidence for your point of view. You need to impart a proven fact that connects with your audience – one they can accept as being truthful. After that, you can present the next proven fact, and so on and so on. It may seem simple, but at times is hard to do. You need a strong belief (and a driving passion) in your point of view with examples of the evidence supporting your conclusions. This can be scientific evidence, in the form of tests, research, accepted theories or facts or even historical evidence based on facts, figures and dates30.

Planning as an integral part of goal setting. Without a plan, reaching your goals tends to be a hit-or-miss proposition, and time is easily wasted. Without a plan, you may find yourself reacting to the demands of others rather than focusing on your own goals. Without a plan, you will miss the benefits that come from using effective planning skills. Before considering the benefits of effective planning, perform the self-audit on the

---

30 Darrin Wiggins. How to Set Goals: Your Goal Setting Bibles for Maximum Personal Achievement, 2013

next page, and identify your strengths and areas for improvement with regard to planning31.

Objective setting is incomprehensible without planning. To accomplish assignments, an individual must arrange certain actions. The result will be fruitful as it were with a clear step-by-step execution of them. At the introductory organize, arranging will not be able to require into consideration all the subtleties, hence, it is conditional. Nevertheless, it is vital since it makes a difference:

- center on truly critical moments;
- determine the bearings in which to move, and the activities taken at the same time;
- eliminate questions and anxiety;
- increase the level of inspiration for the effective accomplishment of the goal;
- determine the activities that have to be performed to realize the result;
- leverage existing abilities and resources;
- self-determination in your claim life;
- gain certainty within the rightness of their claim activities.

The goal setting of an enterprise must follow certain rules:

Goals must be particular and measurable. Accordingly, the result must compare not as it were to the

31 Susan B. Wilson and Michael S. Dobson. Goal Setting: How to Create an Action Plan and Achieve Your Goals,2008

required subjective, but moreover quantitative indicators. Thus, the examination of the accomplishment of objectives, the discernment by the open, and their open dialog are facilitated. As a result, animosity coordinated at the company decreases.

The goals must be relevant to reality, and the enterprise must have the appropriate potential. This is assessed during the cost planning and resource allocation phase. With a lack of temporary potential, employees will not be able to achieve their goals, their trust in management will be lost.

The goals must be loyal to change and able to transform in the process.

Goal-setting must be understandable for all personnel, and goals must be spiritually close to the majority of employees, since their achievement will be a collective activity. Goal setting should be as transparent as possible. This will help analyze the task setting and motivation of employees.

The team must be cohesive, capable of achieving the set goal, regardless of external conditions.

Setting criteria. An effective method for establishing priorities is to use a table. Thei first column identifies your concerns, which may include your goals, current projects, and activities. Subsequent columns identify criteria to evaluate your concerns.

Criteria often used to rank concerns are importance and urgency. With regard to importance, consider the impact of each concern on your goals. Is it an activity of high impact? What impact is likely in terms of cost? Use of resources? What kind of an effect will this activity have on your reaching your goals? As you evaluate your activities using each criterion, assign a number to indicate the level of importance (high = 3, medium = 2, low = 1) and enter this number in the appropriate space of the table

There are five common mistakes when setting goals:

Strategic goals are ignored. Many entrepreneurs prioritize tactical financial challenges. More global goals are often not taken into account. For example, a company plans in the medium term:

- increase the rate of income growth;
- increase profitability;
- increase the amount of cash receipts.

However, the prospects for further development are set precisely by the goals of the strategic plan. The implementation requires significant expenditures of both time and other resources.

Strategic goals can be:

- increasing market share;
- improving product quality;
- work on the reputation of the enterprise;
- increasing the value of the organization.

The goal is formulated in a negative way. A fairly common mistake of goal-setting is associated with the peculiarity of human psychology to avoid the problem, and not get rid of the causes of its occurrence. The definition of the task should be based on the movement towards the result, and not escape from difficulties. Examples of incorrect wording:

- ✓ minimization of risks in a specific area of enterprise activity;
- ✓ reducing the number of employees who are late;
- ✓ reducing the number of complaints.

The goal is formulated vaguely and unclear. Typical examples of vague definitions are: “improving efficiency”, “strengthening labor discipline”, “leadership in this industry”, etc. its departments”. Such a goal is, in principle, unattainable.

Researchers argue that the majority of managers use the concept only to assess the actions of employees. Only 16.6% of managers use the method for its intended purpose - to harmonize the goals of enterprises at different levels. This situation is due to very specific reasons:

6. insufficiently clear formulations of tasks at lower levels;
7. the goals do not express the true needs of the enterprise (they are not aligned with the goals of the upper levels);
8. there are no responsible persons for each direction of goal setting.

The stated goals are not true. Sometimes the leadership voices one goal, but in reality, completely different decisions are made. For example, it is stated: "The interests of the client are above all!"

“My success evolved from working hard at the business at hand every day.” Johnny Carson

Many studies have been conducted over the years to try to determine why it is that some people are more successful than others.

Hundreds, and even thousands of salespeople, staff and managers have been interviewed, tested and studied in an attempt to identify the common denominators of success. One of the most important success factors discovered, over and over again, is the quality of "Action Orientation."32

Thich Naht Hahn: "The path is the goal." In other words, finding your path in life is your goal in life. Your path is not your profession, how much money you make, your title, or your successes and failures. Finding your path means finding out what you were put here on this earth to do. What is your life's purpose? Why were you given this gift called life? And what is the gift you give back to life?33

References:

1. Brian Tracy. Goals! How to Get Everything You Want-Faster Than You Ever Thought Possible,2003
2. Darrin Wiggins. How to Set Goals: Your Goal Setting Bibles for Maximum Personal Achievement, 2013

---

32 Brian Tracy. Goals! How to Get Everything You Want-Faster Than You Ever Thought Possible,2003

33 Robert Kiyosaki. Rich Dad Poor Dad: What the Rich Teach Their Kida About Money That the Poor and Middle Class Do Not! Digest Media, Potpourri ,2012

3. Robert Kiyosaki. Rich Dad Poor Dad: What the Rich Teach Their Kida About Money That the Poor and Middle Class Do Not! Digest Media, Potpourry, 2012
4. Susan B. Wilson and Michael S. Dobson. Goal Setting: How to Create an Action Plan and Achieve Your Goals,2008
5. Хайруллаева, Д.С. Психологическо-дидактические свойства читательской компетенции в подготовке учителя иностранного языка / Д.С. Хайруллаева. — Текст: электронный // NovaInfo, 2022. — № 131. — URL: https://novainfo.ru/article/19051 (дата обращения: 06.04.2022).

www.ingramcontent.com/pod-product-compliance
Lightning Source LLC
LaVergne TN
LVHW010555070526
838199LV00063BA/4983
* 9 7 8 9 3 5 8 7 2 1 3 4 8 *